THE WRITER'S LAB

A PLACE TO EXPERIMENT WITH FICTION

THE WRITER'S LAB

A PLACE TO EXPERIMENT WITH FICTION

WRITER'S DIGEST BOOKS

WritersDigest.com
Cincinnati, Ohio

SEXTON BURKE

For more resources for writers, visit www.writersdigest.com/books.

To receive a free weekly e-mail newsletter delivering tips and updates about writing and about Writer's Digest products, register directly at http://newsletters.fwpublications.com.

16 15   5 4

Distributed in Canada by Fraser Direct
100 Armstrong Avenue
Georgetown, Ontario, Canada L7G 5S4
Tel: (905) 877-4411

Distributed in the U.K. and Europe by F+W Media International
Brunel House, Newton Abbot, Devon, TQ12 4PU, England
Tel: (+44) 1626-323200, Fax: (+44) 1626-323319
E-mail: postmaster@davidandcharles.co.uk

Distributed in Australia by Capricorn Link
P.O. Box 704, Windsor, NSW 2756 Australia
Tel: (02) 4577-3555

Edited by Marielle Murphy
Designed by Claudean Wheeler
Cover Illustration by il67/iStockPhoto.com
Production coordinated by Debbie Thomas

DEDICATION

For my lovely Kate

Welcome, my friend, to "The Lab."

Behind this page lies a fascinating world of experiments, mysteries, and discoveries. You don't need to be a professional writer or have a fancy degree to participate—just keep an open mind and enjoy yourself.

The Lab is a great place to work on your craft. You'll be asked to try new things, write about unusual characters or situations, and overcome challenges regarding your writing skills and creative ingenuity.

But don't let The Lab frighten you! There are no tests here. You can start at page one and work your way through the entire book, or you can choose pages at random—whatever works best for you.

Feel free to write in the book, sketch scenes, tear out entire pages, and start all over again. If you run out of room for a particular challenge, move the story to a separate journal or laptop. The Lab provides a place to start experimenting, but you can finish anywhere you like.

And with that, let's begin.

Good luck!

In the top half of this page, make a list of your favorite books. In the bottom half, detail the qualities that make those books so good. Use the bottom half of this page as a checklist against which to measure your own work. Are you working hard to ensure that your own writing is as good as the literature that inspires you?

Write your first and last name:

Now rearrange the letters and turn them into a new name. Write that name here:

Now write a description of this new person below. You'll use them as a character in a scene on the next page.

On the next two pages, write a scene in which your new character uncovers a secret about his or her family history, including the true meaning of his or her name. End it with a cliffhanger.

5

On the lines below, fill in specific details about the figure provided. For example, what does this person look like? What color is their hair? What do their teeth look like? How do they walk? What kind of clothes are they wearing?

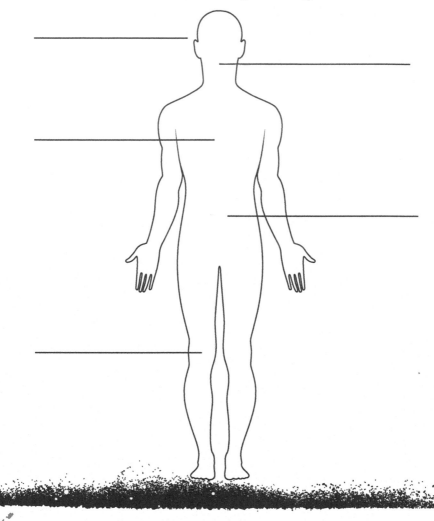

Now, give your character a name and a profession—one that does *not* instinctively fit the physical attributes noted.

Now write a scene in which your
new character's physical attributes actually
enhance his or her professional abilities.

Write a scene during which one character reveals
a powerful and emotional truth to another—
without using any dialogue.

Write a short piece about
the life of a cartoon character.

You are a journalist. Take an incident from
your favorite work of fiction and
rewrite it as a descriptive piece of nonfiction.
Take no sides and convey no bias.

Now take a random news story from today's paper and rewrite it as a work of fiction. Imbue it with a specific point of view.

A man was murdered within a locked room—his personal library. He held the only key. There are no windows, fireplaces, floor grates, or ventilation shafts. The phrase "Better dead than read" is written on his forehead. Who killed him, how, and why?

BETTER
DEAD
THAN READ

Select a fruit or vegetable from your refrigerator. Describe it in the space below. Once finished, write a story with a protagonist who shares those qualities.

TAKE A NAP.
DREAM.

REMEMBER:
YOU HAVE TO DREAM
IN ORDER TO WRITE.

Consider the type of character that
you most often create:

Male/Female

Ethnic background

Social/Economic class

Now write a scene in which the main character
is as far as possible from what you're used to writing,
but keep him or her grounded in reality. Identify
with this new character by thinking
about what you have in common, rather than
the differences that distinguish you.

The suspects have been gathered together and your detective is poised to name the murderer and explain the solution to the mystery. Before doing so, however, he tunes the radio to NPR. Write the scene that explains why.

Your protagonist's car breaks down along a country road late at night. In the distance the protagonist sees another car driving toward him/her very quickly, loud rock music blaring from the windows. What does your protagonist do?

Your protagonist walks in through the front door
and calls out "Honey, are you home?"
All is quiet until a strange voice answers:
"No...Honey's not home." What happens next?

What's in a name? Think about your favorite character from literature and change his or her first or last name.

Write the revised name here:

How does this new name make you reconsider what the character might be like, even if the role of the character stays the same?

The plane is going to crash.
There are 50 seconds until impact—
a LONG time. What do the passengers and
pilots do with that much time?

Think of an argument for which you fully support one specific side. Now write a scene in which you have to fairly—and *successfully*—represent the viewpoint of the opposition.

Try your hand at freewriting. Fill in the remainder of this page with a short story. Write quickly about whatever story comes to mind, without worrying about spelling, grammar, or logic.

Now take the most interesting elements from your freewriting experiment and use them to create a new, carefully written piece on the page above.

Write a brief scene from third person point of view.
The specifics of the scene are entirely up to you.

Write the same scene but this time write it from first person point of view. Once you've finished, turn the page.

Think about any new character details
revealed by writing the same scene in first person
point of view, then rewrite the scene
in third person one last time.
Does the new character information revealed
by the first person draft influence how you craft this
final revision?

Describe the ugliest,
most repulsive setting you can.

Now tell the reader something about
the setting that makes it beautiful.

Write a haiku
(a short poem typically
broken down into three lines
consisting of five, seven,
and five syllables respectively)
that connects these three things:

A ride at an amusement park

An apple

Dreams of childhood

_____

_____

_____

Now write a second haiku that works
as an autobiography. What can you tell the
world about yourself in seventeen
syllables and how elegantly can you tell it?

_____

_____

_____

REST FOR A MINUTE.
RELAX.
HAVE FUN THINKING UP
THE MOST OUTRAGEOUS
PLOT YOU CAN.

WHEN YOU'RE DONE,
TURN THE PAGE.

Now write the scene
that sets that plot in motion.

Put your finger on the object that's closest to your left hand at this moment. Examine it carefully. Write a scene in which this object is the focus of everyone's attention. The reasons why are up to you.

33

Write a scene about a restaurant critic
who loses her sense of taste.

You open the paper one morning to read your own obituary. Shortly thereafter your power shuts off. You try to call a friend but your cell phone doesn't have a signal. What's happening?

On the page above, write a story
about a mystery writer who is asked by a friend
to come up with the perfect murder.

Here's where the plot twists.
Once the plan has been crafted,
your mystery-writing protagonist
begins to suspect that said "friend"
wants to kill her (or him)!

Write a humorous piece of nonfiction about your parents.

Now write it from first person point of view, as if you were one of them.

39

Make a list of everything that irritated you yesterday. Did someone cut you off at a light? Perhaps your spouse forgot to bring home the laundry. Maybe your boss asked you to cancel a lunch date. Make the list complete, including things both large and small.

Something in the list above is about to trigger a murder! Randomly circle one of the choices.

Now write a scene in which one character makes the decision to do away with another character, all because of the triggering incident you circled on page 40. If you want to really challenge yourself, the victim should *not* be the instigator of the triggering incident.

Write a scene of great intimacy,
but with no sex or romantic clichés. In fact,
your characters shouldn't even touch.

It turns out that a young girl's "imaginary friend"
is for real. What happens when the parents find out?

Describe the person
who makes you the most miserable.

Now write about the qualities
that make this person worth loving.

Write a scene from first person point of view.
Your protagonist is blind.

E

F P

T O Z

L P E D

Write the same scene, but this time,
your protagonist is deaf.

Write a haiku from the point of view of a serial killer.

_____

_____

_____

Write a haiku that proves the existence of God.

_____

_____

_____

Create a situation for your protagonist
from which there is absolutely no escape.

Now think of a way out.

In the space above, write a synopsis of your favorite
book. Circle the words that indicate conflict.

Now write a synopsis of your story.
Circle the words that indicate conflict.

Do you find that the conflict driving your story
is as compelling as that of your favorite book?
Would your story be improved by increasing the
points of conflict faced by your protagonist?

Think of a villainous character from literature or film. Write a scene from first person point of view in which he or she is the protagonist. Allow his or her villainous traits to shine through, but remember that the character doesn't think of him or herself as a villain.

Write a joke.
Not a joke you've heard before,
but an original creation.

Now write a scene in which
a character tells this joke and gets
an unexpected response.

Write down the name of your favorite literary character. Make sure the character is one who was alive at the end of the book in which he or she appeared.

Now write a death scene for that character.

Consider the personality traits attributed to
Donald Duck and write them down here:

Now write a scene in which your
protagonist shares those traits.

MAKE A LIST
OF ALL THE THINGS
THAT KEEP YOU FROM WRITING.

WHICH ONE OF THESE
ARE YOU WILLING TO ADMIT
MIGHT BE AN EXCUSE
NOT TO WRITE?

What is your least favorite type of fiction?
Fantasy or romance? Perhaps mystery or horror?
Whatever it may be, name it below and detail
what it is you don't like about the genre.

Now challenge yourself to craft a story in the genre
described above, but avoid all of those things you
dislike. Make this a story that even you have to admit
represents the genre well.

Write a short story about a bold,
courageous superhero (male or female)
who suffers from OCD.

Write the name of your favorite color vertically
along the left hand side of the page. Use each letter
to create a new word starting with that letter.

Now write a poem incorporating
all of the words above.

My men, like satyrs
grazing on the lawns,
Shall with their goat-feet
dance an antic hay.

From *Edward II* by Christopher Marlowe

Take the scene suggested by this classic verse
and re-envision it in a contemporary setting.

Write down one line from your favorite song.

Now write a scene in which the words of this song take on an entirely different meaning.

Write a modern-day "Tower of Babel" story.
What happens and what are the implications?

Test your descriptive powers by selecting
one item, person, or setting and describing it three
times. Each description should be accurate, yet
completely different, with no shared details.

Of these three classic monsters, Dracula, The Wolfman, and Frankenstein, two (vampires and werewolves) have been turned into romantic figures in both literature and film. Write a short story that makes the Frankenstein monster into a romantic figure.

Write a scene in which one person observes the death of another.

Now write a scene in which someone observes a birth.

71

In the year 2036, a law is passed that requires doctors to manipulate the genetic code of unborn children to ensure that they are born without any physical "defects." Write a story in which a parent argues for the right to allow their child to be born naturally.

Write a story that ends exactly where it begins.

Scientists suddenly discover that Pluto has vanished.
What happened to it and why? Write the story.

A fire rages throughout an apartment building. There's one person left inside. When an opportunity to get down the stairs presents itself, this person opts to stay right where they are. Write a story that explains why.

Write a scene around an emotional conflict, but refrain from using any words containing the letters "C" or "M."

Take your most frightening memory
from childhood and write a story in which the memory
takes on even more horrifying dimensions.

In the top half of this page, write a list of five things that are most important to you. Circle one of them.

In the space below, describe how the loss of that one circled thing would change your life.

Write a short story in which your protagonist loses that which is dearest to him or her. Try to capture the depth of emotion you would feel, given a similar loss.

Write down the title of the worst book
you've ever read.

Describe what the author did wrong and how you
would have improved the story.

Always remember to spend time analyzing your
own work with as much objectivity.

GO OUTSIDE.

LOOK FOR SOMETHING UNEXPECTED.

STAY THERE UNTIL YOU SPOT IT.

- - - - - -

NOW GO BACK IN AND TURN THE PAGE.

Write a story about the unexpected thing
that you saw outside. This thing should radically
change your protagonist's life.

You're on a crowded subway car during rush hour. Across the aisle you see an astonishingly attractive man, though it's not his appearance that's so compelling. You must get to know this man before his stop arrives. How do you make it happen? Write the scene.

Write a short story in which the following three things play an important (and logical) role in the plot:

A scarecrow

Egypt

Nail clippers

If "story" = "physics,"
what = "gravity?"

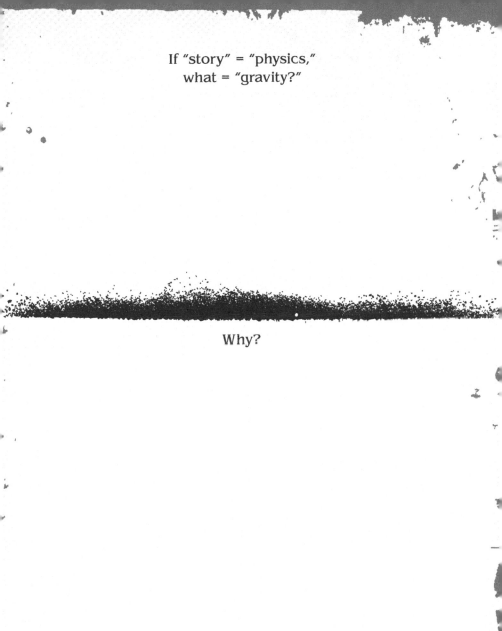

Why?

Create a character of Shakespearean proportions. What makes them amazing? What do they look like? How do they appear to those around them? Fill in the chart below with character defining details.

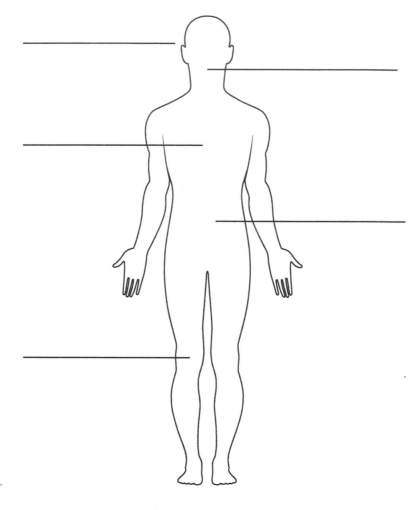

Now, what is their fatal flaw?

Using the character created on the previous page,
write a scene in which everything is going his or her
way until that fatal flaw comes into play.

Pull six of your favorite novels off the shelf and place them face up in front of you, ordered 1 through 6. Roll a die. Write down the name of the protagonist from the book indicated by the resulting number. Roll the die again and write down a one sentence summation of the plot from the book indicated.

Now write a short story adapting the plot from the book indicated, but replacing the protagonist from that story with the one indicated by your first die roll.

If you could see the future, but—like Cassandra of ancient Greek myth—no one believed you, what would you do? What if a loved one's life depended on you being able to convince someone?

Write a scene in which your protagonist
must obtain a particular object, but the object
is guarded by that which he fears the most.

Make an anagram out of your first and last
name in order to create the name of a fictitious author.
Write the jacket copy for a book written by this
fabulous new author below. What kind of book
would he or she write?

In the spaces above, try your hand at drawing comic strips. These strips can be crude, of course, but think about how the images progress from panel to panel in order to convey time passing and movement. Are you a skilled enough storyteller to present a narrative through images?

Create two characters that have a symbiotic relationship. The pairing of Clarice Starling and Hannibal Lecter is a good example.

Now write a scene in which one of your two characters finds that he or she no longer needs the other.

Roll a six-sided die. The number rolled equals
the number of characters in your scene. Get them
all talking and work hard to make each voice distinct.
(If you roll a 1, roll again.)

Describe the nature of time and space in a haiku.

_____

_____

_____

Write a haiku that explains how to write a poem.

_____

_____

_____

Your protagonist walks through the door
into a dark room. Suddenly the lights come up and
someone yells "Surprise!" What happens next is a
comedy of errors. Write the scene.

Imagine what would have happened to Dorothy Gale of Kansas if she'd made it into the storm cellar before the tornado hit. Write the story.

You wake up one morning with the ability to levitate objects with your mind, but only if they weigh no more than an ounce or two. Above this paragraph, detail how you would use this newfound ability for good. Below, detail how you would use it for evil.

Think of a character from a story that you've written. Now create a secret for that character that puts his or her actions in a whole new light. Write down the details of the secret.

How does this new secret affect your thoughts about this character? How might it affect reader perception?

Take on the role of your favorite fictional
character and write a short essay in their voice.

Think about your day yesterday. What happened that would make the kernel of a good story? If you can't think of something right away, give it some time. Think about conflicts, accidents, misunderstandings, mistakes, etc. Once you have an idea, start writing the opening scene that begins that story.

In his book *On Writing*, Stephen King recommends the formula 2nd Draft = 1st Draft − 10%. In other words, do yourself a favor by streamlining the narrative and trimming the fat from your work. With that rule in mind, take one of the stories you've written elsewhere in The Lab and rewrite it here, trimming the word count by at least 10%.

Write a scene in which your protagonist receives an envelope with no return address. What's in it? How does your protagonist react to the contents and why?

"CONSISTENCY IS THE LAST REFUGE
OF THE UNIMAGINATIVE"
—OSCAR WILDE

IT'S EASY TO WRITE THE SAME TYPE
OF STORY AGAIN AND AGAIN.
PUSH YOURSELF
TO TRY SOMETHING NEW.

Look out your window and select one
object or creature (not another person) that's within
view. Write down all of the physical
characteristics of your selection. Now write a
short story featuring a protagonist who has
those same characteristics.

Think of a story that you've been working on
that you've not been able to finish.
Do you know how it ends? If so, write the
ending below. Don't know how it ends? Take a deep
breath and write an ending anyway.

Once you've got an ending, go back to where you
stopped writing originally and see if that new ending
helps you to finish the rest of the piece.

Write a scene in which one person tells
another about their deepest, darkest secret.

Write that same scene again, but this time, from the point of view of the person hearing the secret.

In most fiction, the protagonist achieves his or her desires one way or another. Write a story in which the protagonist comes close to succeeding, but ultimately fails. Can you write this scene in such a way that it's still satisfying for the reader?

Let's say God returns to Earth in human form. Write about his first day back. If a conflict arises that suggests a larger story, continue writing.

Write a story about a woman who wakes up,
goes into the bathroom, and finds seven adult teeth
in her medicine cabinet.

Create an insufferable character for your protagonist to deal with. Throughout the course of your story, detail the circumstances that ultimately drive them together. What changes do the characters have to go through in order to make this relationship work?

In *The World Without Us*, Alan Weisman posits
what would happen to the Earth if all humans
disappeared in an instant. Now it's your turn to
complete the story. What happened to us?

A woman loses her husband in a horrible accident. She buries him, only to find out years later that he was never who she thought he was. Write the circumstances behind this deception and what she does upon finding out.

Write a poem in free verse. It should fill up this entire page.

Write a children's picture book about
one of these four topics:
loneliness, adventure, love, or **individualism.**
Rather than trying to draw anything,
include a description of each illustration.

In the space above, list all of your negative qualities.
Be honest. Once finished, create an honorable
character in the space below who shares the qualities
that you've listed above. Save this amazing character
for an important story.

Write about an artist who loses one of her hands in an accident. Whenever she thinks about painting, she's struck by an odd "phantom limb" sensation.

Think about the worst thing you've ever done. Write a scene in which your protagonist does the exact same thing, but feels totally different about having done it.

Write a scene in which a truth is exposed as a lie and that revelation reveals a lie that is actually true.

Consider the opening paragraph
from Dashiell Hammett's *The Maltese Falcon*:

*Samuel Spade's jaw was long and bony, his chin a
jutting v under the more flexible v of his mouth. His
nostrils curved back to make another, smaller, v.
His yellow-grey eyes were horizontal. The v motif
was picked up again by the thickish brows rising
outward from twin creases above a hooked nose,
and his pale brown hair grew down—from high
flat temples—in a point on his forehead. He looked
rather pleasantly like a blond satan.*

A vivid portrayal of the protagonist, wouldn't you
say? Write a scene in which an important character is
drawn just as vividly. Use whatever method of doing
so you prefer: description, dialogue, action, etc.

You receive a package in the mail. The card with the package wishes you well on your wedding day, but you're not getting married. Write the story of what's really going on.

Write about a brief, violent encounter
in first person present tense.

Think about the very first story you can remember writing – the farther back in your memory the better. Now rewrite that story using every writing skill you've picked up since then.

Write a scene that takes place in "slow motion" so that you can record every detail as it happens.

Have you captured anything in this extended description that you wouldn't have thought about had the scene played out at "normal" speed?

Write James Bond as if the character was—
and always has been—a woman.

In your scene, how did this change affect the way the character acted or spoke—if indeed it did?

Do you think the change made the character more compelling, less compelling, or essentially the same?

What characters have you created recently that might benefit from a little reinvention?

Give your protagonist an impossible challenge—one that they refuse to recognize as impossible.

Think of your favorite writer and his or her style of
writing. Mimic it as best you can on the page above.

In the space above, draw a map. In the space below, write a description of the most important location on this map and tell us why it's so important.

Now write a scene that takes place in this important location and use the rest of the landscape on the map to inform how the characters look, feel, and interact with one another.

Write a scene in which everything
is conveyed through dialogue.

Before you do anything else today, fill this
page from side to side and top to bottom with every
word or phrase you can think of that describes
how you feel about your lover.

In the 1930s, pulp magazines were the most popular reading material of the day. They could be adventurous, romantic, horrifying, lurid, or out of this world—sometimes all at once. Write a short story that contains all of those elements, without sacrificing literary quality for the sake of outrageousness.

Write a haiku that solves a crime.

_____

_____

_____

Write a haiku that makes no sense to anyone but you.

_____

_____

_____

Go online and conduct an image search
using the term "modern art." Select one of the results
at random. This image is the jacket cover for your
new book. Now write some jacket copy for the story
suggested by this cover image.

Try your hand at some world building. By this we don't necessarily mean world building as in "Mars," but if your protagonist lives on a different planet, or dimension, that's perfectly fine. In the broader sense, think about the world inhabited by your protagonist. Use this page to sketch out the major elements of this world that influence his or her personality (political scene, culture, social environment, etc.), even if it's not something you make explicit in your story.

Now write a short piece in which the influence of these elements are evident in your protagonist's actions (or lack thereof) without directly referencing them.

Write yourself into a corner.

Write a short piece in which your favorite romantic hero spends an afternoon doing something incredibly mundane.

Are the hero's established personality traits evident even though he's doing something that he's not typically associated with?

Consider the butterfly effect. A butterfly flaps its wings in one location and causes a car wreck on the other side of the world due to the sequence of events that result from that initial action. Write a story in which a seemingly insignificant event has a life-altering effect upon one of your characters.

Write a scene in which a single young woman finds a baby abandoned in the back seat of her car.

Using the same inciting incident, re-write that scene with a young man as your protagonist.

Think about how much writing time you've lost during the past month due to procrastination. Now write a short piece about the book you *would* write if you could get that lost time back.

What are you doing next month?

While on Noah's Ark, you discover that someone is eating the animals. Solve this horrifying crime!

Write a dialogue-heavy scene in which
only one person is present.

MAKE UP A LIST OF
FIVE FICTIONAL BOOK TITLES.

KEEP THE LIST UNTIL AT LEAST ONE
OF THOSE BOOKS IS A REALITY.

Ian Fleming was a master at describing leisure activities, from eating to playing cards. Write a scene in which your protagonist does very little of apparent interest. Your job is to make it interesting.

You wake up one morning to discover that you have small butterfly wings growing out of your ankles. Write the story that explains what's happening.

Take the plot of your favorite novel and reconceptualize it as middle grade (ages 8-12) fiction. Write a description of that new book here:

Can you retain the elements that make the novel great without "dumbing it down" for a younger audience?

Now do the reverse.

Take a middle grade novel and reenvision it as an adult novel. Write the description here:

Did you feel the need to complicate the story
or did it hold up as originally written?

The "quest" is a well known plot archetype. Write a quest story that not only fulfills the standards of a quest, but also offers an opportunity for character transformation as the quest is fulfilled.

Zombies have been integrated into normal society. Write a short story in which it's evident that "domesticated" zombies are much more terrifying than the alternative.

In the space above, write a paragraph describing what motivates your character on a daily basis. In the space below, write a paragraph detailing the incident that forces your character to abandon that which motivates him or her.

Write a story about the next stranger
who sits across from you.

Write a flashback. Use that flashback to inspire
the story it's flashing back from.

Write down the title of your favorite book:

Now make a list of every way that you think
the book could be improved.

Perfection is not required of great fiction. Don't allow
the need for perfection to inhibit your writing.

Write a short piece of adventure fiction
with literary sensibilities.

Many have tried to guess what the woman portrayed in da Vinci's Mona Lisa was thinking when he painted her. Write the story that explains it all.

Write about what happened to you yesterday as if you
were writing a piece of genre fiction.

Write about a natural disaster that forces
a diverse group of people to work together (or not)
in order to survive.

Write a scene from first person point of view
of a spirit viewing a séance.

In J.R.R. Tolkien's classic *The Hobbit*, the tragic Gollum challenges Bilbo Baggins to a deadly game of riddles. Bilbo wins the game simply by asking Gollum "What have I got in my pocket?"

Check your pocket then write a short mystery— a kind of riddle, really—in which whatever you found in your pocket is part of the solution.

TAKE A SHORT BREAK FROM WRITING AND
READ SOMETHING EXTRAORDINARY.

In *The Odyssey*, Odysseus escapes the Cyclops by blinding the monster's single eye. Write a story in which your protagonist defeats his or her enemy by exploiting a less obvious "blind spot."

Write about a romantic encounter that ends in
tragedy, but for only one of the characters.

In Alfred Hitchcock's suspense masterpiece
North by Northwest, Cary Grant's character, Roger
Thornhill, waits at an isolated crossroads where
he expects to learn crucial insights about what's
happening and why. It's one of the most suspenseful
scenes in cinema even though much of the scene is
spent waiting for something to happen.

Write a scene in which you focus on
ratcheting up the suspense without resorting
to cheap shocks or scare tactics.

A "meet cute" is film terminology for a scene in which two characters meet for the first time and a romantic connection is made. The scene—a staple of romantic comedies—is typically humorous and, well, cute.

Write a meet cute for your romantic duo, but do it in such a way that neither character realizes what's happening until it's too late to do anything about it.

Write about a day in the life of God.

Write about a day in the life of the Devil.

179

Dream up an antagonist for a future story and make a list of his or her predominant character traits – the more villainous the better.

Now write a story featuring a protagonist that shares those same traits.

Have someone read your story when it's finished.
Is the protagonist sympathetic?

Write a scene in which a gravedigger
uncovers something unexpected while preparing
for an upcoming funeral.

In the space above, write a death scene.
In the space below, start writing the story that
leads to that death scene.

After dozens of experiments, every good scientist draws some conclusions. Fill this page with your thoughts about writing, why you love it, why it makes the world a better place, and why *your* work deserves to be read by others.

Sexton Burke is an author and publisher. Under another name he has written or co-written three books devoted to the craft of writing, as well as numerous articles for writing and journaling magazines. He can currently be seen as a background player in the H.P. Lovecraft Historical Society's new film *The Whisperer in Darkness*. He lives with his wife in Brooklyn, New York.

NEVER STOP EXPERIMENTING!

The Writer's Idea Book, 10th Anniversary Edition

BY JACK HEFFRON

Once a writer has an idea, what then? Ideas without a plan, without a purpose, are no more than pleasant thoughts. This revised, updated, and expanded new edition will help you find the answers. With more than 800 thought-provoking prompts and exercises, you'll generate intriguing ideas and turn them into amazing works of prose!

Question of the Day

BY AL KATKOWSKI

Are you an explorer of ideas? If so, then this is the book for you. The questions inside are designed to generate fun, enlightening, surprising, or revealing answers. It's an ideal ice breaker among acquaintances or a source of deeper conversation for old friends. No matter the answer, you're guaranteed to get that much closer to what's real.

Both of these titles and more are available from **WritersDigestShop.com** and your favorite book retailers.